This is P

Its Buildings and their Story

Researched and written by Geoffrey Place
Drawings by Michael Barton
Cover painting by David Scott

Second Edition
Reprinted with amendments

Parkgate Society
2008

Published by
Parkgate Society

ISBN 978 0 9534964 0 2

First edition 1979
Reprinted 1992
Second edition 1999
Reprinted with amendments 2008

Second edition designed and typeset
by David Morris

Printed in Great Britain by
EWS Colour Print Ltd, Buckley

Buildings described in the book

Samuel William Ryley (c.1756–1837),
Actor-manager and Parkgate resident

Parkgate's story is one of change, from the woods and grassland of a deer park, through a century of fame as a port for shipping and as a resort for seabathing, to years of decline as a fishing village. Its fortunes revived when it became a residential area, and the village now relies on its power to attract both residents and visitors. Part of that power is its unusual history.

Parkgate's name derives from Neston Park, which was enclosed about 1250 and served as a deer park for 350 years. The river shore beside Neston Park was recorded as one of several anchorages where ships would unload their goods if they were too large to reach Chester. In 1610 a sailor was arrested for smuggling some calfskins, which were being exported without the necessary licence, from Chester through Parkgate — the first use of this name so far discovered.

From the 1680s passenger ships began to call at Parkgate, and a village began to grow. Until 1815, Parkgate was renowned as a terminal for packet ships taking passengers to and from Dublin. Travellers of all types, from the Lord Lieutenant of Ireland to Irish harvesters, would wait here for a favourable wind.

From 1760 to 1830, Parkgate was also well known as a resort where people came to take the seabathing cure, for their health rather than for fun.

Parkgate died as a port because the main stream of the river, which used to run on the English side, was forced by the hand of man to run on the Welsh side. This started by the building in 1737 of the New Cut, which canalized the river for five miles below Chester. The change in the course of the river was completed by 1815.

Parkgate struggled to survive as a fishing village, but was given new life by the coming of the railway in 1866. The tide came in twice a day until about 1940. The marsh then spread rapidly, and the fishermen moved down river. The marsh in front of Parkgate is now a bird reserve, visited by many thousands of migrant waders and wildfowl.

Parkgate became a Conservation Area in 1973, a status which protects the historic charm of an unusual place — a charm which draws hosts of visitors to the Parade every fine day.

For route and location of buildings, see the plan on Pages 18 and 19.

The road from Neston to Parkgate was made a turnpike, or toll road, in 1787. Before that, the way to Parkgate was down Moorside Lane and along the shore.

The **pillbox** (Plan, 1) was built as a machine-gun emplacement in 1939 to defend the railway bridge in case German paratroops landed on the estuary. The pillbox was never used, but several German airmen did come ashore at Parkgate after baling out of their stricken planes.

The pillbox in Station Road

Parkgate's first **railway station** (Plan, 2) was built in 1866 at the end of a single-track line from Hooton. Its site is now a car park. In 1886 the line was extended to West Kirby, and a new station was built on the other side of the road, to allow for a goods yard where the old station had been. The railway not only brought trippers and encouraged commuters to live here, but took Parkgate's fish, especially shrimps and shellfish, to market. The line was closed to passenger traffic in 1956 and the track was taken up eight years later. In 1969 the twelve-mile route of the railway became the Wirral Country Park.

The red-brick former stationmaster's house stands next to the **Neston and District Cricket Club** (Plan, 3), founded in 1895 by Dr Henry Speechly. The original wooden pavilion was burned down in 1971 and replaced by a new clubhouse and squash courts.

Cheltenham Place

Dr Speechly was the first resident of the topmost house in the row of houses opposite the cricket ground, originally called **Cheltenham Place** (Plan, 4) after the nearby Cheltenham Walk, now called the Ropewalk. These houses, together with Sandheys (see pp.21, 24), were the first in Parkgate to have the black and white decoration which has since spread throughout the village. The Ropewalk was made about 1814 so that seabathing visitors had somewhere to walk when the weather was rough on the Parade.

The **Station Road cottages** (Plan, 5) include two houses of historic interest. Dover Cottage — the one nearest the river, Number 16 — is said to be the house where Emma Lyon lodged in 1784 when she came to take the seabathing cure for a skin complaint. It was the house of Mrs Downward, "a lady whose husband is at sea". Emma found it decent, comfortable and quiet, but expensive. Emma later became Lady Hamilton and famous as the lover of Admiral Nelson.

The eighteenth-century cottages in Station Road

Emma's letters from Parkgate shed light on the way the seabathing cure was undertaken. "The sea water has done me so much good. I have drunk a tumbler glass every morning, walked half an hour, then bathed and breakfasted. I have the tang [seaweed] applied to my knees and elbows every night going to bed, and wash them twice a day in the sea water. And they are just well."

Next door is **Nelson Cottage**, which is not called after the admiral, but after a small boy called Nelson Burt. The house was the weekend cottage of Albin Burt, a Chester painter who specialized in miniature portraits. In December 1822 Albin Burt was returning from Liverpool to Chester with his nine-year-old son Nelson. They boarded the paddle steamer *Prince Regent*, intending to travel on the Mersey to Ellesmere Port and then by canal to Chester. A severe storm arose and the steamer ran out of coal. It tossed about for six hours, and in the darkness nine people, including young Nelson, were swept overboard and drowned. When the sorrowing father next visited Parkgate, he collected some black pebbles from the beach and set them in the ground in front of his cottage to spell out his son's name as a memorial. In the 1920s they were set in cement to preserve them.

Look at the very narrow house, Number 13. There used to be a passage here, between its neighbours, and this house was squeezed into the gap.

The oldest houses are the ones nearest the river, though none was here when a map was drawn in 1732. Numbers 16, 15, 14, and 11 date from the eighteenth century. At the other end, Numbers 1 to 5 were built in 1852, and the rest filled in the spaces at other times to complete the row (Plan, 6).

Nos 7, 6 and 5, Station Road, c.1980

The Old Quay Inn with its car park was built in 1963, but its site used to contain some houses of interest. The next drawing shows the houses that used to stand opposite the Station Road cottages. On the left was the **Chester Hotel**, (Plan, 7), an inn since the 1850s, and the house on the right, nearest the river, had once been the **Parkgate Custom House** (Plan, 8).

"To be sold at the Parkgate Custom House," reported the Chester newspaper in 1778, "Irish printed muslin, cotton and linen, brandy, rum, geneva, rectified spirits of wine, and Bohea tea, which goods have been seized and condemned." There are records of several other auctions of smuggled goods at 'the Long Room' of the Custom House.

In 1791 Jane Reilly recorded in her diary that she was rowed ashore from her ship, the *Princess Royal*, and was carried across the wet sands by sailors. "We found a chaise on the beach to take us to the inn where we dressed as soon as we could get the luggage from the Custom House." The Customs ceased to use this house in 1821, and withdrew completely from Parkgate in 1828.

Houses formerly on the site of the Old Quay Inn

Aerial view of South Parade in 1930

The aerial view of **South Parade** as it was in 1930 shows the South Slip (Plan, 9), with its fifteen steps. Over half these steps, and over half the height of the sea wall, have since been covered by the rising saltmarsh.

Although Parkgate was an important anchorage throughout the eighteenth century, there was then no sea wall, no landing stage, no quay and no road between the houses and the beach. The present sea wall was not built for the benefit of shipping. Its middle section was built about 1800 as a parade for the fashionable visitors who came for the seabathing season. A Chester newspaper reported in 1811:

"A grand, brilliant and splendid display of fireworks will be exhibited on the shore beneath the Terrace at Parkgate on Saturday 10th August."

The south end of the sea wall, from the Donkey Stand (see p.23) to the South Slip, was built about 1830. The north end, from the Watch House to the Boat House, was built in the 1840s, and called the New Marine Parade.

Seaward House, on the left

Here are several interesting buildings of the early eighteenth century, when a great deal of building took place locally. All three houses were described as "new" in 1732, and they were probably all built in the 1720s. These three, together with some thirty other buildings in Parkgate, are listed as buildings of special architectural or historical interest.

Seaward House (Plan, 10) carries a date plate of 1721. Since it was drawn, the bow windows, which are not original, have been extended upwards. For some fifty years after about 1870 the house was a boarding school for young boys. Several private schools were set up at Parkgate at different times in the nineteenth century, partly because the sea air was considered healthy. Both schools and lodging houses were an important part of the economy, as

Prospect House, with Talbot House on the right

Parkgate was not a prosperous fishing village. In 1841, out of 235 employed adults, only thirteen were fishermen, although there were 25 by 1871, when the railway was making the catch more marketable.

12

Next to Seaward House is **Talbot House** (Plan, 11). This building was the Talbot Inn between at least 1764 and 1808. It is said that Mrs Fitzherbert, the estranged wife of the Prince Regent, later George IV, stayed at the Talbot to enjoy the sea air in 1798 or 1799. She is said to have taken pity on soldiers who were camping on the shore while waiting to suppress a rebellion in Ireland, and to have paid for extra rations for them.

In 1772 Alexander Kirkpatrick wrote in his diary, "Went on board the *Britannia* at 9.15 a.m. on Wednesday, and landed at Parkgate at 9.30 on Friday morning. Breakfasted at the Talbot." This journey of 48 hours from Dublin was slow; fifteen hours was thought a good time.

The house on the left in the drawing, **Prospect House**, seems always to have been a private residence, and behind it is a very small cottage intended for servants. Its bay windows, which appear distinctively antique, were in fact added in the 1860s. Bay windows were clearly fashionable then, as they were added to the original box-like fronts of Seaward House, the Ship Inn and Alma Cottage at about the same time.

The rather overwhelming façade of **Mostyn House** (Plan, 12) dates from 1932, when the eighteenth-century front wall was in danger of collapse and had to be strengthened. Its earlier appearance can be seen in the next drawing. Here was the George Inn, dating certainly from 1770, and possibly from 1750. Its landlord in 1770 was Joseph Manlove, who also had bathing machines on the beach.

Manlove's son-in-law, Thomas Spencer, ran the George Inn for twenty years, until he decided in 1808 that Parkgate was declining and that he should move to the Eagle & Child at Holyhead. He was right, as the packet ships did fade away, but the George survived. Its landlady, Esther Briscoe, reopened it as the Mostyn Arms Hotel in 1819, enlarged and fitted up in the first style of elegance.

Esther Briscoe ran her hotel with great success for a further thirty years. When the whole village was sold in 1849, she bought her own hotel, but by that time Parkgate's seabathing was no longer popular in the face of competition from New Brighton. When Mrs Briscoe died in 1855 there was no market for the building as a hotel, and it was taken by a schoolmaster, Edward Price. He transferred his school from Tarvin to Parkgate in the summer of 1855 and called it Mostyn House School.

Mostyn House in 1880

In 1862 Price transferred the school to his nephew, the Rev. A. S. Grenfell. By then the building was old and in poor condition, and when the horrified Mrs Grenfell first saw it, she declared, "I had never seen such a horrible hole in all my life." The building was then owned by Thomas Brassey, the railway contractor, because he had provided Mrs Briscoe's mortgage in 1849. Brassey died in 1870 and A. S. Grenfell was then able to buy the freehold of the property.

He left Parkgate in 1882, and for seven years the headmaster was William Barrett, curate of Neston and a former head boy of the school.

In 1890 A. S. Grenfell's eldest son, Algernon (A. G.) Grenfell, became headmaster of Mostyn House. The building was in bad condition, and to save the school he had to change its appearance and character. He greatly increased its size and made it a preparatory school — a school taking boys between the ages of 8 and 13, and preparing them to go to public schools. It was a sign of A. G. Grenfell's confidence that, when he had succeeded in building the school's numbers from 20 to 100 in five years, he was able to build a fine **chapel** (Plan, 13). He was his own architect for this impressive building. It was opened in 1897, and contains an interesting set of stained glass windows, including seven by Robert Anning Bell (1863–1933). Next

14

Mostyn House School Chapel

to the chapel is a carillon of 37 bells, installed as a war memorial to those of the school's Old Boys who fell in the First World War. The sound of these bells is familiar to every resident of the district.

In 1985 Mostyn House changed its character again to become a wholly day school. It now has a nursery, as well as departments for infants, juniors, seniors and a Sixth Form.

The **water tower** (Plan, 14) is another Parkgate landmark. It was built in 1906 to support a water tank which is fed from the school's own artesian well. The drawing shows the tower as it was when first built, before other buildings were added at its base.

The water tower

Mostyn House was the birthplace in 1865 of Sir Wilfred Grenfell, A. G. Grenfell's brother. Wilfred went to the Labrador coast of Canada in 1892 and became renowned for his pioneering work among the poverty-stricken fishermen there as a medical missionary. As a boy he had loved the outdoor life on the Dee estuary.

15

W. T. Grenfell, 1865–1940

As a man he relished the challenge of an inhospitable coast and climate, as well as the dedication of serving his fellow men. An incident in 1908 which made him famous, and described in his book, *A Labrador Doctor*, related to his crossing the frozen waters of a Newfoundland bay in a sledge, when the ice began to break up. He survived a night of bitter cold by killing three of his husky dogs and wrapping their skins round him. He placed a memorial tablet in the Mostyn House chapel which reads, "In grateful memory of my rescue from a drifting ice-floe and of three brave dogs, Moody, Watch and Spy, whose lives were sacrificed to save mine."

Mostyn House in 1970

Between Mostyn House and the Ship Hotel there used to be an alley (locally called a weint) called Drury Lane. Up Drury Lane there was a coach house used as a temporary theatre during Parkgate's seabathing days. The playbills survive for several plays performed here in the summer of 1811.

The building now comprising the Ship used to be at least three houses — in front was the post office (in 1850), behind that the Ship Inn and behind that another inn called the Bull's Head.

The **Ship Inn** (Plan, 15) was first known by the name of an actual ship, the *Princess Royal*. This ship was built at Parkgate in 1787 by the Parkgate Packet Company to carry passengers to Dublin. It was last recorded here in 1808, and was sailing out of Liverpool in 1810. Like most ships using Parkgate, it was quite small (133 tons), with two masts and a single deck. The inn was rebuilt and enlarged to enclose most of the left side of Drury Lane in 1860, and reopened as the Union Hotel. Over a century was to pass before the hotel reverted to its former name, the Ship.

To the left of the hotel, where a bar has since been built, there used to stand Hilbre House, also shown in the drawing, demolished in the 1960s.

Hilbre House and the Ship Hotel in 1930

The building containing **Nicholls'** and the post office (Plan, 16) was built in 1935 on the site of a building called Dee House. William Kingsley ("King") Nicholls was a Neston dairyman who built an ice cream parlour whose product has been justly famous ever since.

Parkgate

Wirral
Cheshire

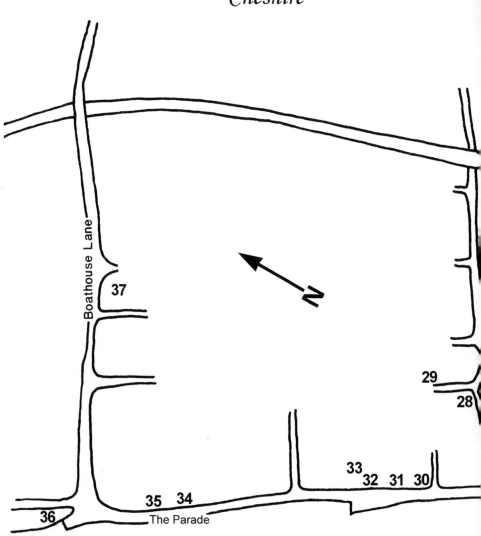

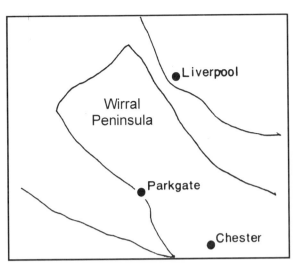

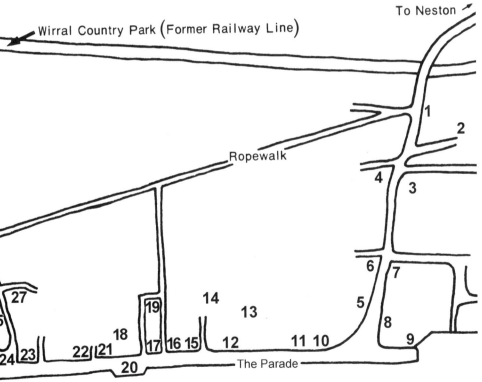

To Neston

Wirral Country Park (Former Railway Line)

Ropewalk

The Parade

River Dee

Nicholls' ice-cream shop

Parade House in 1975

Between Nicholls' and **Parade House** (Plan, 17) is Little Lane, a more modern weint than Drury Lane because it was created in 1849. Go up it to see the two houses behind Parade House. They are small houses crammed into the smallest possible space, typical of early Parkgate. Parade House, built in the early eighteenth century, used to be private houses.

Balcony House (Plan, 17) was built about 1750 as two houses. Some thirty years later a very large room was added at the rear (you can see it behind the north side), and this was the Assembly Room. Visitors for the seabathing

Balcony House before repair in 1996

would pay a shilling to join, and could then enjoy coffee, the newspaper, a meal, sometimes card parties and dances. For another shilling a gentleman could play billiards. In 1808 George Harrison, "master of the Billiard room at Parkgate, married Widow Grimes, head bathing woman to the ladies who frequent the place. He was a married man, a widower and a bridegroom within three weeks." When Harrison died in 1814 he was described as "a most lively and eccentric character".

After the seabathing visitors had deserted Parkgate, the Assembly Room was used for occasional public gatherings, but in the 1880s became part of the house in front. In 1995 the Assembly Room, threatened with demolition, became a separate dwelling.

The elegant iron balcony which gives the house its modern name was erected in 1868. During the Second World War, the cellar of the house was reinforced for use as an air raid shelter.

South Cottage

South Cottage (Plan, 17) is the attractive house on the south side of Balcony House. Before 1851 part of this building jutted out into the roadway and was the White Lion Inn. The inn bore a date plate of 1708.

Alma Cottage (Plan, 18) was named after the battle of the Alma river in the Crimea, 1854. When the entire village of Parkgate was sold in 1849, the owner (Edward Lloyd Mostyn) offered this site, then empty, for the building of a church. But nobody was prepared to pay for one, and Henry Platt, a Chester chemist, built a house for himself here in 1855.

Between Balcony House and Alma Cottage there runs a lane called Holywell Close. At its end may be seen the four black and white houses called **Sandheys** (Plan, 19). They were built in 1900 at the same time and by the same architect as Cheltenham Place (see p.7). The Sandheys houses were originally called Playground Place because they were built on part of the sports field of Mostyn House. This area used to be known, before it was built on, as The Green, and before the First World War people danced here after the annual regatta. "First race was with the sails, then the race with oars in the punts; while that was going on the band would be playing. After the boat races they would have a tug of war between the fishermen of Parkgate and Neston, then they would have races for children." This was the memory of one such child, Mrs E. M. Hough, who won a prize.

Alma Cottage

Opposite Alma Cottage there is a bastion of the sea wall known as the **Donkey Stand** (Plan, 20). A house used to stand there, a tall, narrow building which was the only exception to the saying, "All on one side like Parkgate." The house served as the first Assembly Room and was then converted into sea-water baths, "hot and cold, for the convenience of invalids, with an outlet for those who prefer the open sea". The first stretch of sea wall had to go round this house's foundations, thus creating the bastion when the house was demolished in 1840. After 1871 when Bank Holidays were introduced, donkeys used to stand here and take children for rides to the South Slip and back for 2d. One little girl was frightened because her donkey went so fast!

Holywell House (Plan, 21) was built in 1863 as two 'villas'. A sketch of the "large, roomy, old-fashioned house" which was demolished to make way for these villas was made by William Herdman, the Liverpool artist. In 1918 the two villas were combined and run as the Holywell Hotel for thirty years. In recent times it has become residential flats.

Sandheys

Next to Holywell House is **The Warren**. This house was rebuilt in 1906, but its predecessor, looking much the same, can be seen in Herdman's painting. From at least 1832 John Salkeld ran his "Classical and Commercial Academy" here, with eighteen resident boy pupils. The school came to an end when Salkeld retired in 1861.

The house to the right of the Red Lion, called Clontarf, was the post office in the 1870s, and later bore the sign, "Thomas Nelson, grocer, provision dealer". Between the wars it was a café.

The **Red Lion** (Plan, 22) is the oldest of the surviving Parkgate pubs to have remained unchanged. First recorded in 1822, the Wood family ran it for the rest of that century. In Parkgate's days as a passenger port, local innkeepers used some sly tricks to gain custom. A traveller in the 1740s, who had been induced to leave his Chester inn by the untrue report of a fair wind at Parkgate, complained, "I have learned at Parkgate that it is a common custom of the publicans there to send up false intelligence to Chester; that

The Warren and Holywell House

The Red Lion

the company may come down to lie under the lash of their long bills."

The group of houses which are shown on the next page (Plan, 23) illustrate how many of the Parkgate houses looked in the eighteenth century — starkly functional before being given bay windows and dormers in the nineteenth century, and black and white paint in the twentieth. The drawing shows them as they were in 1890. Sea View, the house on the right edge of the drawing, has been dated by English Heritage inspectors to about 1750, though many changes have been made since then.

Teal Cottage, Seven Steps, "the butcher's shop" and Sea View

The name of **Mostyn Square** (Plan, 24) commemorated the Mostyn family of North Wales, who owned the entire village of Parkgate and most of Neston from 1672, when Thomas Mostyn married Bridget Savage, heiress to these lands, until 1849, when their great-great-great-grandson sold all his Cheshire estates at auction. Although the Mostyns lived in Wales they seemed to have worked for Parkgate's benefit. In 1821 the last baronet, Sir Thomas, reduced the rents of his tenants by 25% and wrote to his agent "to remember his poor tenants — he considered himself and them all of one family, and if they suffered, he suffered also."

The road running uphill beyond Mostyn Square was the boundary between the ancient townships of Great Neston to the south and Leighton to the north. It was also "the great double ditch" of Neston Park. In medieval times the land to the north was Leighton Wood.

St Thomas's (Plan, 25), "a neat Gothic building" as the Directories of Cheshire used to put it, is interesting for its windows, which have iron glazing bars in petal patterns. It was built in 1843 as a Congregational chapel, partly at the expense of a visitor from Yorkshire, George Rawson. The chapel relied heavily on summer visitors for its upkeep and was heavily in debt when a Liverpool sugar merchant and keen Presbyterian, R. A. Macfie, came to live nearby. Macfie bought the Parkgate chapel and it was converted to Presbyterian worship in 1858. When a new Presbyterian church was built nearer Neston in 1884, this chapel was used only for occasional concerts until the Church of England leased it in 1910. They bought it seven years later and named it after St Thomas.

St Thomas's

Behind the church is the **Old School House** (Plan, 26). It was built as an infants' school in 1860 and served the children of Parkgate for 107 years until replaced by a new primary school 400 yards up the road. Although it was usually a happy and effective school, the original design was unsatisfactory: "The roof is thin and consequently the room is very cold in winter and hot in summer, the ventilation is distinctly defective and the light is poor", wrote the inspector in 1904. Notice the attractive pattern of the slate roof.

Parkgate infants' school (now Old School House)

Beyond the school are **Coastguard Cottages** (Plan, 27), running parallel to the river. They were built in 1858 when the Royal Navy took over the coastguard service and reorganized it, apparently not realizing that Parkgate

Coastguard Cottages

was no longer a port. Four coastguards and their families were installed here, with nothing whatever to do, until 1875. When Wilfred Grenfell and his brother were boys, they used to listen to the coastguards' tales of smugglers, and would purloin ancient cartridges from their boathouse and extract loose gunpowder for use on their duck-hunting expeditions.

On the other side of the road, in School Lane, is **Mostyn Cottage** (Plan, 28), probably built in the 1790s. There was a public house on its left side in 1818. In the 1860s William Barrie ran a small boarding school at Mostyn Cottage with about ten boys, and he called it Parkgate Academy.

Mostyn Cottage

The three houses **Leighton Banastre**, **Banastre Cottage** and **Brockleigh** (Plan, 29) are set back from the bustle of the Parade in the quiet of their own park-like grounds. They were built between 1791 and 1795 by the Liverpool architect George Cripps. They were built as four houses, and converted into three in the 1850s. Originally all these houses, with a group in School Lane, were called Mostyn Place.

The southernmost house, now called Brockleigh, was a girls' boarding school for at least fifty years. In 1810 a Mrs Tomlinson

Leighton Banastre

advertised her school for young ladies in Mostyn Place. And in 1817, "Young ladies may be accommodated for the Bathing Season only at 15s. per week, education included." The last principal was Elizabeth Sellers, who retired in the 1860s.

Leighton Banastre is one of at least three houses in Parkgate where it has been claimed that Handel stayed in 1741 on his way to Dublin for the first performance of the Messiah. In this case the claimant could not have known that the house was built fifty years too late. In fact we know from the Dublin newspapers that Handel did not reach there from Parkgate, but from Holyhead. Handel did pass through Parkgate on his return in August 1742, but there is no reason to suppose that he stayed here.

As you pass along the Parade past Mostyn Square, you may buy the shrimps for which Parkgate has long been famous. It was about 1940 that the local fishermen found that the rising marsh stopped them keeping their boats here. There used to be an annual supper for the fishermen at the Masonic Hall behind the Union Hotel. One year a prize was offered for the biggest lie, and John Mealor urged his cousin, John Peters, to enter. "I've never told a lie in my life", said Peters. "Give him the prize!" cried Mealor — and he got it, a copper kettle.

Overdee and Grey Walls

Overdee and **Grey Walls**, with their neighbour **Maple Cottage** (Plan, 30), make an interesting group of eighteenth-century houses. The sea wall has no parapet here, and in the fishing days nets were hung to dry on the railings.

The Moorings (Plan, 31) is one of only two houses on the Parade which has a gable end facing the river.

The Moorings

Further along is the Middle Slip, where donkey carts, and later lorries, used to collect the catch brought by the fishing boats.

Trains used to leave Parkgate station with cockles and mussels bound for Lancashire and Yorkshire.

The saltmarsh in front of Parkgate is part of the Gayton Sands Reserve of the Royal Society for the Protection of Birds, which bought 5,000 acres of the estuary in 1979.

The Watch House (Plan, 32) was apparently built in the 1720s. The house was originally two rooms, one on top of the other, joined by an outside stone stair. In 1799 it was leased by the Customs as a lodging for their officers and a place to keep watch on shipping at the other end of the

The Watch House

village from the Custom House. The Customs ceased to use it in 1828, when they leased it to Mary Cunningham, bath house keeper.

Beyond the Watch House there stands on the bank a white house which was built on the site of, and apparently also incorporates, an ancient cottage known locally as **Ryley's Castle** (Plan, 33). It was the home of an actor, Samuel Ryley (c.1756–1837).

31

He loved his tiny "Cottage of Content". "My small residence stands on an eminence, the base of which is washed by the returning tides of the river Dee. The Welsh mountains on the opposite shore, six miles distant, form an amphitheatre extending north and south, and when the tides come in it covers an expanse of at least twenty miles, and presents one of the finest views imagination can conceive."

Ryley's Castle

Ryley was a romantic who eloped with his employer's daughter and married her 'across the anvil' at Gretna Green. He is known to have acted at Parkgate in 1812 and 1815. He was a very popular man, despite being chronically in debt. When imprisoned for debt in 1813 he complained, "Without any previous demand I was dragged from my peaceful domicile at Parkgate." The drawing of him on Page 4 comes from his autobiography, published in no fewer than nine volumes.

The large house behind a stone wall, now called **Brooke House** (Plan, 34) was built for his own use in 1903–4 by the architect W. Aubrey Thomas, who designed the Liver Building in Liverpool. He was a Dickens enthusiast and called it Bleak House. He had three beautiful daughters, and he raised the wall so that they could sit in the garden without being ogled by all the passers-by.

Sawyers Cottage and **Pengwern** (Plan, 35) were built together, about 1700, or a few years before. **Dee Cottages** were built later in the eighteenth century, and the whole group was at one time referred to as Pengwern Place. Sawyers Cottage was a public house, the Sawyer's Arms, until 1905. Its original landlord from c.1793 to 1822 was Richard Bartley, a sawyer and carpenter. The house has a brick-vaulted 'cellar' above ground, to keep the beer cool.

Dee Cottages, Sawyers Cottage and Pengwern

Dee Cottages used to suffer from damp and flooding when the tide came over the sea wall. Perhaps it was here in 1802, after a storm which "at Parkgate was unusually severe, scarcely a house being habitable, an old woman was unfortunately drowned in her bed."

There was an inn on the site of the **Boat House** (Plan, 36), called simply the Beer House, as early as 1620. It became known as the Ferry House, or Boat House, when a ferry sailed between here and Flint. Two women were drowned in 1799 when a ferry boat overturned while trying to race another. In 1813 Richard Ayton had an uncomfortable crossing: "We took our passage together with a crowd of other passengers, being packed and crammed into our places with as little regard for our ease in such a state of stowage as though we had been dead cargo." A coach used to meet the ferry to take passengers to the Mersey ferries or, after 1840, to Hooton station. In 1864 Thomas Johnson, the landlord of the inn, was drowned with his brother Joseph while trying to land in rough weather.

The inn, known latterly as the Pengwern Arms, was pulled down about 1885 after storm damage. The site lay empty until a café was built here in 1926. The drawing dates from that time. The café was enlarged in 1977 to become a restaurant and then a public house.

The Boat House

Further down the shore an open-air swimming pool was in use between 1923 and 1950. Its site has become a popular picnic area for the Wirral Country Park.

On the shore near the Boat House there was in the eighteenth century a boatbuilder's yard. One ship built here, the *Duke*, is known to have carried slaves from Africa to Jamaica in 1754. Three passenger ships for the Parkgate Packet Company were built here: the brigs *King*, *Queen* and *Princess Royal*.

When Thomas Makin, the shipwright of these three, went bankrupt in 1790, he had eight apprentices.

The **Parkgate Hotel** (Plan, 37) was built as a private house in 1860 by Joseph Rich. He called it Richville: unwisely, as he was bankrupt three years later. In about 1918 May Richardson moved her girls' school here and called it Leighton School. She retired in 1939 when the building was requisitioned by the Army. It became a hotel after the war until 2000, when private houses were built on the site.

From a point a little higher up Boathouse Lane, J. M. W. Turner painted the view of Flint Castle across the estuary. As Samuel Ryley wrote, "Need I say the sight was grateful? Aye, none more delightful in all the round world."

FURTHER READING

Geoffrey Place, *The Rise and Fall of Parkgate, Passenger Port for Ireland, 1686–1815* (Chetham Society, 1994)

Geoffrey Place (ed.), *Neston 1840–1940* (Burton and South Wirral Local History Society, 1996)

Geoffrey Place (ed.), *Neston at War 1939–1945* (Burton and South Wirral Local History Society, 1999)

Parkgate Society

Parkgate Society, which has published this guidebook, was founded in 1972. Its first task then was to counter the proposal to build a barrage and bridge across the estuary just down river from Parkgate, and huge reservoirs to be held by high earth banks in front of the village. Fortunately this plan proved too expensive.

We believe that Parkgate's unique character is well worth preserving, and our next task was to advise on the formation of the Conservation Area, which now covers all the buildings in Parkgate that lie close to the estuary.

Over the years, the society has worked to enhance Parkgate, for example by planting trees and daffodils, by publishing and promoting its history, and by keeping an eye on its interests and speaking out when necessary. We maintain close links with our local councillors and officials of the borough council and with our MP.

For our members we arrange a programme of talks, nearly all of local interest, from September to May. Twice a year a newsletter is sent to each member.

If you would like more information about Parkgate Society, please enquire at Neston Library, where the staff can put you in touch with our secretary.